직장인, 유학 준비생, 손글씨가 필요한 모두를 위한

영어필기체
쉽게쓰기
100

직장인, 유학 준비생, 손글씨가 필요한 모두를 위한

영어필기체
쉽 게 쓰 기
100

초판 1쇄 발행   2016년 9월 26일
초판 17쇄 발행 2025년 3월 14일

지은이 시원스쿨어학연구소
펴낸곳 (주)에스제이더블유인터내셔널
펴낸이 양홍걸 이시원

홈페이지 www.siwonschool.com
주소 서울시 영등포구 영신로 166 시원스쿨
교재 구입 문의 02)2014-8151
고객센터 02)6409-0878

ISBN 979-11-86858-50-9 13740
Number 1-010202-22222600-02

이 책은 저작권법에 따라 보호받는 저작물이므로 무단복제와 무단전재를 금합니다. 이 책 내용의 전부 또는 일부를 이용하려면 반드시 저작권자와 ㈜에스제이더블유인터내셔널의 서면 동의를 받아야 합니다.

영어필기체쉽게쓰기100문장

직장인, 유학 준비생, 손글씨가 필요한 모두를 위한

영어필기체 쉽게쓰기

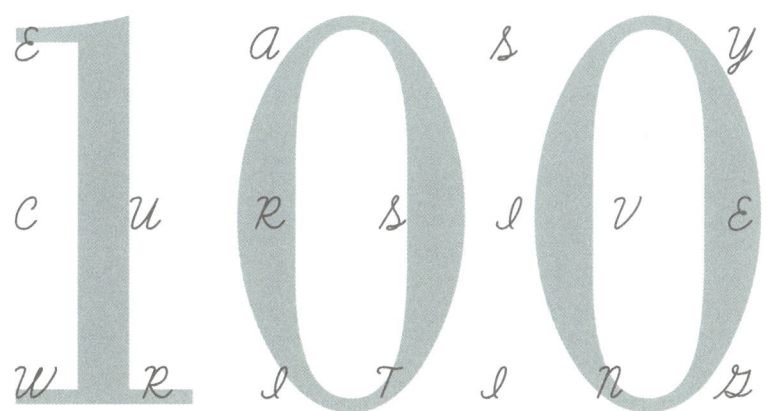

시원스쿨닷컴

이 책 쓰는 법

1 영어 필기체에 꼭 필요한 선긋기와 알파벳 이어쓰기로 **영어 필기체 쓰기를 위한 준비**를 하세요.

2 본격적으로 각 **알파벳이 들어간 단어들을 연습**합니다. 중학교 수준의 단어들로 구성되어 부담 없이 단어와 영어 필기체를 동시에 익힐 수 있습니다.

3 편지, 영어 일기 등 **쓰기에 필요한 주요 문장 100문장**을 연습해 보세요.

4 <셰익스피어의 작품> 속 명문장과 <어린왕자>를 영어 필기체로 쓰면서 **고전과 문학 작품을 감상**해 보세요.

5 영어 필기체를 활용하기에 좋은 **서명 연습, 다양한 형태의 필기체**를 연습해 보고 자신감을 향상시키세요.

차례

1 **Warm-up** 선 긋기 연습 — 8

2 **Warm-up** 알파벳 써 보기 — 9

3 **Step 1** 단어 써 보기 — 10

4 **Bonus 1** 한국인의 가장 흔한 성 써 보기 — 38

5 **Bonus 2** 가장 흔한 남자 이름 써 보기 — 40

6 **Bonus 3** 가장 흔한 여자 이름 써 보기 — 42

7 **Step 2** 문장 써 보기 — 44

8 **Step 3** 문학작품 써 보기 — 76

9 **Bonus 4** 카드, 편지를 위한 예쁜 필기체 써 보기 — 94

C 대문자 미리보기
apital Letters

A	B	C	D
E	F	G	H
I	J	K	L
M	N	O	P
Q	R	S	T
U	V	W	X
Y	Z		

Small Letters
소문자 미리보기

a	b	c	d
e	f	g	h
i	j	k	l
m	n	o	p
q	r	s	t
u	v	w	x
y	z		

Warm-up

[선긋기 연습] 필기체 쓰기에 필요한 선들을 충분히
연습하고 필기체를 쓸 준비를 하세요.

[알파벳 이어쓰기]

알파벳을 따로 써 보고 연결해서
익숙해지도록 충분히 연습해 보세요.

ABCDEFGHIJKLMNOPQRSTUVWXYZ

abcdefghijklmnopqrstuvwxyz

ABCDEFGHIJKLMNOPQRSTUVWXYZ

abcdefghijklmnopqrstuvwxyz

영어필기체쉽게쓰기100문장

|단어 써보기|

알파벳 A 쓰기

A a a

a
a

1 A가 **맨 앞**에 오는 단어를 연습해 보세요.

action
action 행동

action

aim
aim 목표, 겨누다

aim

admit
admit 인정하다

admit

2 A가 **중간**에 오는 단어를 연습해 보세요.

react
react 반응하다

react

attach
attach 첨부하다

attach

private
private 사적인

private

3 A가 **맨 뒤**에 오는 단어를 연습해 보세요.

extra
extra 여분의

extra

flea
flea 벼룩

flea

zebra
zebra 얼룩말

zebra

B 알파벳 B쓰기

1 B가 **맨 앞**에 오는 단어를 연습해 보세요.

blanket
blanket 담요

billion
billion 10억

beggar
beggar 거지

2 B가 **중간**에 오는 단어를 연습해 보세요.

debt
debt 빚

tube
tube 관, 튜브

bubble
bubble 거품

3 B가 **맨 뒤**에 오는 단어를 연습해 보세요.

grab
grab 잡아채다

lab
lab 실험실

rub
rub 문지르다

알파벳 C쓰기

C C c

C

c

1 C가 **앞**에 오는 단어를 연습해 보세요.

conduct
conduct 수행하다

conduct

coal
coal 석탄

coal

client
client 의뢰인, 고객

client

2 C가 **중간**에 오는 단어를 연습해 보세요.

cancel
cancel 취소하다

cancel

accurate
accurate 정확한

accurate

force
force 힘, 강요하다

force

3 C가 **맨 뒤**에 오는 단어를 연습해 보세요.

genetic
genetic 유전(자)의

genetic

panic
panic 공포, 패닉

panic

electronic
electronic 전자의

electronic

D 알파벳 D쓰기

D d

1 D가 **맨 앞**에 오는 단어를 연습해 보세요.

detail
detail 세부 사항

delay
delay 미루다

duty
duty 의무, 세금

2 D가 **중간**에 오는 단어를 연습해 보세요.

adopt
adopt 입양하다

midnight
midnight 자정

ladder
ladder 사다리

3 D가 **맨 뒤**에 오는 단어를 연습해 보세요.

acid
acid 산성

method
method 방법

grand
grand 웅대한

알파벳 E쓰기

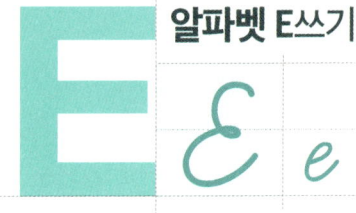

1 E가 **맨 앞**에 오는 단어를 연습해 보세요.

exit
exit 출구, 나가다

employ
employ 고용하다

erase
erase 지우다

2 E가 **중간**에 오는 단어를 연습해 보세요.

fee
fee 요금, 수수료

cruel
cruel 잔인한

swear
swear 맹세하다

3 E가 **맨 뒤**에 오는 단어를 연습해 보세요.

tongue
tongue 혀

ache
ache 아픔, 통증

wipe
wipe 닦아내다

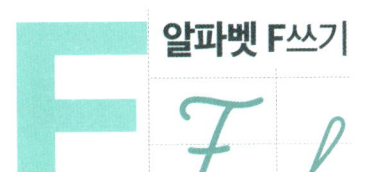

알파벳 F 쓰기

1 F가 **맨 앞**에 오는 단어를 연습해 보세요.

- *faint* faint 희미한
- *fortune* fortune 큰 돈, 행운
- *flame* flame 불꽃

2 F가 **중간**에 오는 단어를 연습해 보세요.

- *refresh* refresh 기운나게 하다
- *differ* differ 다르다
- *refuse* refuse 거절하다

3 F가 **맨 뒤**에 오는 단어를 연습해 보세요.

- *proof* proof 증거
- *thief* thief 도둑
- *deaf* deaf 귀가 먼

G

알파벳 G 쓰기

$\mathcal{G}$ g

---

1 G가 **맨 앞**에 오는 단어를 연습해 보세요.

guilty
guilty 죄책감을 느끼는

gap
gap 틈, 격차

grave
grave 무덤

2 G가 **중간**에 오는 단어를 연습해 보세요.

regret
regret 후회하다

rough
rough 거친, 대략의

delight
delight 기쁨

3 G가 **맨 뒤**에 오는 단어를 연습해 보세요.

plug
plug 플러그, 마개

hug
hug 포옹하다

jog
jog 조깅하다

알파벳 H쓰기

H h

---

1 H가 **맨 앞**에 오는 단어를 연습해 보세요.

hire
hire 고용하다

handle
handle 다루다

harsh
harsh 가혹한, 거친

2 H가 **중간**에 오는 단어를 연습해 보세요.

chef
chef 주방장

chase
chase 쫓다

shell
shell 조개 껍질

3 H가 **맨 뒤**에 오는 단어를 연습해 보세요.

sigh
sigh 한숨짓다

punish
punish 벌하다

high
high 높은

알파벳 I 쓰기

l   i

l
i

1 I가 **맨 앞**에 오는 단어를 연습해 보세요.

iron
iron 철, 다리미 — *iron*

illusion
illusion 환상 — *illusion*

ideal
ideal 이상적인 — *ideal*

2 I가 **중간**에 오는 단어를 연습해 보세요.

insist
insist 주장하다 — *insist*

crime
crime 범죄 — *crime*

senior
senior 연장자 — *senior*

3 I가 **맨 뒤**에 오는 단어를 연습해 보세요.

ski
ski 스키 — *ski*

alibi
alibi 알리바이, 변명 — *alibi*

taxi
taxi 택시 — *taxi*

알파벳 J 쓰기

𝒥
𝒿

1 J가 **맨 앞**에 오는 단어를 연습해 보세요.

joke
joke 농담(하다)

joke

jewel
jewel 보석

jewel

justice
justice 정의

justice

2 J가 **중간**에 오는 단어를 연습해 보세요.

major
major 주요한, 전공

major

enjoy
enjoy 즐기다

enjoy

subject
subject 과목, 주제

subject

영어 필기체 소문자를 이어서 써 보세요.

abcdefghijklmnopqrstuvwxyz

abcdefghijklmnopqrstuvwxyz

K 알파벳 K 쓰기

K K k

K
k

1 K가 **맨 앞**에 오는 단어를 연습해 보세요.

knee
knee 무릎

knee

kingdom
kingdom 왕국

kingdom

kind
kind 친절한

kind

2 K가 **중간**에 오는 단어를 연습해 보세요.

awake
awake 깨어있는

awake

like
like 좋아하다

like

darkness
darkness 어둠

darkness

3 K가 **맨 뒤**에 오는 단어를 연습해 보세요.

risk
risk 위험

risk

leak
leak 새다

leak

task
task 과업, 임무

task

알파벳 L 쓰기

1 L이 맨 앞에 오는 단어를 연습해 보세요.

laugh 웃다

loud 큰소리의

leisure 여가, 레저

2 L이 중간에 오는 단어를 연습해 보세요.

chalk 분필

pale 창백한, 옅은

plenty 많음, 충분함

3 L이 맨 뒤에 오는 단어를 연습해 보세요.

spoil 망치다

steel 강철

wheel 바퀴

알파벳 M 쓰기

M m

m
m

1 M이 **맨 앞**에 오는 단어를 연습해 보세요.

mud
mud 진흙
mud

military
military 군사의
military

minor
minor 중요하지 않은
minor

2 M이 **중간**에 오는 단어를 연습해 보세요.

comic
comic 희극의, 웃기는
comic

dumb
dumb 멍청한
dumb

permit
permit 허락하다
permit

3 M이 **맨 뒤**에 오는 단어를 연습해 보세요.

charm
charm 매력, 매혹하다
charm

germ
germ 병균, 싹
germ

jam
jam 잼, 막힘
jam

N 알파벳 N쓰기

𝓃 𝓃

𝓃

1 N이 **맨 앞**에 오는 단어를 연습해 보세요.

nail
nail 손톱, 못

nail

net
net 그물

net

nod
nod 끄덕이다

nod

2 N이 **중간**에 오는 단어를 연습해 보세요.

lunar
lunar 달의

lunar

laundry
laundry 세탁물

laundry

tiny
tiny 아주 작은

tiny

3 N이 **맨 뒤**에 오는 단어를 연습해 보세요.

chain
chain 사슬, 연쇄점

chain

drown
drown 익사하다

drown

lean
lean 기대다

lean

O

알파벳 O쓰기

O O o

O
o

1 O가 **맨 앞**에 오는 단어를 연습해 보세요.

odd
odd 이상한, 홀수의

odd

occur
occur (일이) 일어나다

occur

obey
obey 따르다

obey

2 O가 **중간**에 오는 단어를 연습해 보세요.

bomb
bomb 폭탄

bomb

double
double 2배의

double

doubt
doubt 의심하다

doubt

3 O가 **맨 뒤**에 오는 단어를 연습해 보세요.

volcano
volcano 화산

volcano

hero
hero 남자 영웅

hero

zoo
zoo 동물원

zoo

P 알파벳 P쓰기

P p
P
p

---

1 P가 **맨 앞**에 오는 단어를 연습해 보세요.

pill
pill 알약

profit
profit 이익

process
process 과정

2 P가 **중간**에 오는 단어를 연습해 보세요.

propose
propose 제안하다

apply
apply 지원하다

rapid
rapid 매우 빠른

3 P가 **맨 뒤**에 오는 단어를 연습해 보세요.

dump
dump 내버리다

snap
snap 딱 부러지다

sharp
sharp 날카로운

Q 알파벳 Q 쓰기

1 Q가 **앞**에 오는 단어를 연습해 보세요.

quit
quit 그만두다

quality
quality 품질

quick
quick 빠른

2 Q가 **중간**에 오는 단어를 연습해 보세요.

request
request 요청하다

liquid
liquid 액체(의)

square
square 정사각형의

영어 필기체 소문자를 이어서 써 보세요.

abcdefghijklmnopqrstuvwxyz

알파벳 R쓰기

R
r

1 R이 **맨 앞**에 오는 단어를 연습해 보세요.

rank
rank 계급, 지위

rent
rent 임대하다

rate
rate 비율

2 R이 **중간**에 오는 단어를 연습해 보세요.

pure
pure 순수한, 맑은

concern
concern 걱정, 관심

salary
salary 봉급

3 R이 **맨 뒤**에 오는 단어를 연습해 보세요.

solar
solar 태양의

anger
anger 화

sour
sour (맛이) 신

알파벳 S쓰기

1 S가 **맨 앞**에 오는 단어를 연습해 보세요.

skin
skin 피부, 가죽

skin

steam
steam 증기

steam

sunset
sunset 일몰

sunset

2 S가 **중간**에 오는 단어를 연습해 보세요.

poison
poison 독, 독살하다

poison

bless
bless 축복하다

bless

assist
assist 돕다

assist

3 S가 **맨 뒤**에 오는 단어를 연습해 보세요.

crisis
crisis 위기

crisis

address
address 주소, 연설

address

happiness
happiness 행복

happiness

알파벳 T쓰기

1 T가 **맨 앞**에 오는 단어를 연습해 보세요.

- **trade** trade 매매
- **tend** tend 경향이 있다
- **train** train 기차

2 T가 **중간**에 오는 단어를 연습해 보세요.

- **faith** faith 신뢰, 신앙
- **strict** strict 엄격한
- **satisfy** satisfy 만족시키다

3 T가 **맨 뒤**에 오는 단어를 연습해 보세요.

- **profit** profit 이익을 얻다
- **arrest** arrest 체포하다
- **twist** twist 비틀다, 꼬다

U 알파벳 U 쓰기

1. U가 **맨 앞**에 오는 단어를 연습해 보세요.

universe
universe 우주

usual
usual 보통의

urgent
urgent 긴급한

2. U가 **중간**에 오는 단어를 연습해 보세요.

purchase
purchase 구입하다

fuel
fuel 연료

junior
junior 연소자의

3. U가 **맨 뒤**에 오는 단어를 연습해 보세요.

flu
flu 독감

menu
menu 메뉴

adieu
adieu 안녕, 작별인사

V 알파벳 V 쓰기

$\mathcal{V}$ v

1　V가 **맨 앞**에 오는 단어를 연습해 보세요.

victory
victory 승리

version
version (개정)판

valuable
valuable 귀중한

2　V가 **중간**에 오는 단어를 연습해 보세요.

devil
devil 악마, 마귀

flavor
flavor 맛

clever
clever 영리한

영어 필기체 소문자를 이어서 써 보세요.

abcdefghijklmnopqrstuvwxyz

알파벳 W쓰기

1 W가 **맨 앞**에 오는 단어를 연습해 보세요.

wealthy
wealthy 부유한

wood
wood 나무, 목재

wage
wage 임금

2 W가 **중간**에 오는 단어를 연습해 보세요.

sweat
sweat 땀을 흘리다

owe
owe 빚을 지다

switch
switch 바꾸다, 스위치

3 W가 **맨 뒤**에 오는 단어를 연습해 보세요.

sew
sew 바느질하다

row
row 노를 젓다

chew
chew 씹다

알파벳 X 쓰기

$\mathcal{X}$

x

1 X가 **맨 앞**에 오는 단어를 연습해 보세요.

xylophone
xylophone 실로폰

x-mas
x-mas 크리스마스

x-ray
x-ray 엑스레이

2 X가 **중간**에 오는 단어를 연습해 보세요.

export
export 수출(하다)

expression
expression 표현

exhibition
exhibition 전시(회)

3 X가 **맨 뒤**에 오는 단어를 연습해 보세요.

tax
tax 세금

fix
fix 고치다

index
index 색인

Y

알파벳 Y쓰기

1 Y가 **맨 앞**에 오는 단어를 연습해 보세요.

yawn
yawn 하품하다

yell
yell 소리치다

yet
yet 아직, 이미

2 Y가 **중간**에 오는 단어를 연습해 보세요.

voyage
voyage 긴 항해

gym
gym 체육관, 체조

payment
payment 지불(액)

3 Y가 **맨 뒤**에 오는 단어를 연습해 보세요.

annoy
annoy 짜증나게 하다

holy
holy 신성한

curly
curly 곱슬곱슬한

알파벳 Z쓰기

1 Z가 **맨 앞**에 오는 단어를 연습해 보세요.

zone
zone 지대, 구역

zero
zero 숫자 0

zip
zip 지퍼

2 Z가 **중간**에 오는 단어를 연습해 보세요.

citizen
citizen 시민, 국민

dozen
dozen 다스[12개]

horizon
horizon 수평선

3 Z가 **맨 뒤**에 오는 단어를 연습해 보세요.

quiz
quiz 퀴즈

waltz
waltz 왈츠

buzz
buzz 윙윙거리다

Bonus1

[한국인의 가장 많은 성]

한국인의 가장 많은 성을
필기체로 연습하고 사인 등에 활용해 보세요.

Kim
Kim 김

Lee
Lee 이

Park
Park 박

Choi
Choi 최

Jung
Jung 정

Kang
Kang 강

Cho
Cho 조

Yoon
Yoon 윤

Jang
Jang 장

Lim
Lim 임

Oh	*Oh*
Oh 오	
Han	*Han*
Han 한	
Shin	*Shin*
Shin 신	
Seo	*Seo*
Seo 서	
Kwon	*Kwon*
Kwon 권	
Hwang	*Hwang*
Hwang 황	
Ahn	*Ahn*
Ahn 안	
Song	*Song*
Song 송	
Ryu	*Ryu*
Ryu 류	
Hong	*Hong*
Hong 홍	

Bonus2

[많이 쓰는 남자 영어 이름]   많이 쓰는 남자 영어 이름을
필기체로 연습하고 사인 등에 활용해 보세요.

Noah
Noah 노아

Liam
Liam 리엄

Mason
Mason 메이슨

Jacob
Jacob 제이콥

William
William 윌리엄

Ethan
Ethan 이든

James
James 제임스

Alexander
Alexander 알렉산더

Michael
Michael 마이클

Benjamin
Benjamin 벤자민

Elijah
Elijah 엘리야

Daniel
Daniel 대니얼

Aiden
Aiden 에이든

Logan
Logan 로건

Matthew
Matthew 매튜

Lucas
Lucas 루카스

Jackson
Jackson 잭슨

David
David 데이비드

Oliver
Oliver 올리버

Jayden
Jayden 제이든

Bonus3

[많이 쓰는 여자 영어 이름] 많이 쓰는 여자 영어 이름을
필기체로 연습하고 사인 등에 활용해 보세요.

Emma
Emma 엠마

Olivia
Olivia 올리비아

Sophia
Sophia 소피아

Ava
Ava 에이바

Isabella
Isabella 이자벨라

Mia
Mia 미아

Abigail
Abigail 아비가일

Emily
Emily 에밀리

Charlotte
Charlotte 샬롯

Harper
Harper 하퍼

Madison
Madison 매디슨

Amelia
Amelia 아멜리아

Elizabeth
Elizabeth 엘리자베스

Sofia
Sofia 소피아

Evelyn
Evelyn 에블린

Avery
Avery 에이버리

Chloe
Chloe 클로이

Ella
Ella 엘라

Grace
Grace 그레이스

Victoria
Victoria 빅토리아

영 어 필 기 체 쉽 게 쓰 기 1 0 0 문 장

|문장써보기|

생활 영어 필수 문장 20

안부 묻고 답하기

1

How have you been?

How have you been? 어떻게 지냈어요?

How have you been?

2

Long time no see.

Long time no see. 오랜만이에요.

Long time no see.

3

How's your family?

How's your family? 가족들은 안녕하세요?

How's your family?

4

Let's keep in touch.

Let's keep in touch. 계속 연락합시다.

Let's keep in touch.

감사/사과 표현하기

5 *Thank you for your help.*
Thank you for your help. 도와주셔서 감사합니다.

6 *I couldn't be happier.*
I couldn't be happier. 더 기쁠 수가 없어요.

7 *I'm sorry for everything.*
I'm sorry for everything. 여러 가지로 죄송합니다.

8 *It's not a big deal.*
It's not a big deal. 별거 아니에요.

응원/격려 표현하기

9

I'll do my best.

I'll do my best. 최선을 다해 볼게요.

I'll do my best.

10

You're doing great.

You're doing great. 당신은 잘 하고 있어요.

You're doing great.

11

Think on the bright side.

Think on the bright side. 긍정적으로 생각해 보세요.

Think on the bright side.

12

I'm sure you can do it.

I'm sure you can do it. 당신이 할 수 있다고 확신해요.

I'm sure you can do it.

대화 할 때 필수 표현

13

Are you following me?

Are you following me? 이해가 되세요?

Are you following me?

14

That's a good idea.

That's a good idea. 좋은 생각이에요.

That's a good idea.

15

I'll get to the point.

I'll get to the point. 요점을 말씀 드릴게요.

I'll get to the point.

16

Let's talk about something else.

Let's talk about something else. 우리 다른 얘기 해요.

Let's talk about something else.

약속잡기/만나기

17

What time can we meet?

What time can we meet? 몇 시에 만나는 게 좋으세요?

What time can we meet?

18

Anytime is okay with me.

Anytime is okay with me. 아무 때나 괜찮아요.

Anytime is okay with me.

19

I had a good time.

I had a good time. 좋은 시간이었어요.

I had a good time.

20

You made my day.

You made my day. 덕분에 최고의 하루를 보냈어요.

You made my day.

영어 필기체 쉽게 쓰기 100문장
자유롭게 적어보기

특별한 날 편지 쓰기 20

생일/크리스마스 편지

1

Happy birthday to you.

Happy birthday to you. 생일 축하해.

Happy birthday to you.

2

Best wishes for your 20th birthday.

Best wishes for your 20th birthday. 20번째 생일을 축하해.

Best wishes for your 20th birthday.

3

Merry Christmas and Happy New Year!

Merry Christmas and Happy New Year! 즐거운 성탄과 행복한 새해되세요!

Merry Christmas and Happy New Year!

4

Happy holidays.

Happy holidays. 행복한 연휴되세요.

Happy holidays.

사랑/우정의 편지

5

I can't stop thinking about you.

I can't stop thinking about you. 나는 당신 생각을 멈출 수가 없어요.

I can't stop thinking about you.

6

I love you more than anything.

I love you more than anything. 난 너를 세상 무엇보다 사랑해.

I love you more than anything.

7

I love you with all my heart.

I love you with all my heart. 나는 당신을 진심으로 사랑해요.

I love you with all my heart.

8

Thank you always being my friend!

Thank you always being my friend! 항상 나의 친구로 있어 줘서 고마워!

Thank you always being my friend!

스승의 날/어버이날 편지

9

I wish you a happy Teachers' Day.

I wish you a happy Teachers' Day. 행복한 스승의 날 되시기 바랍니다.

I wish you a happy Teachers' Day.

10

You are the best teacher in this world.

You are the best teacher in this world. 선생님은 세상 최고의 선생님이십니다.

You are the best teacher in this world.

11

Thank you for being my Mom!

Thank you for being my Mom! 저의 엄마로 있어 주셔서 감사해요!

Thank you for being my Mom!

12

Happy Parents' Day!

Happy Parents' Day! 어버이 날 축하드려요!

Happy Parents' Day!

축복의 편지

13

Wish you all the happiness in the world.

Wish you all the happiness in the world. 세상의 모든 행복을 소망합니다.

Wish you all the happiness in the world.

14

Joy, Love & Laughter!

Joy, Love & Laughter! 기쁨, 사랑, 웃음이 함께 하기를!

Joy, Love & Laughter!

15

I bet you can make it.

I bet you can make it. 네가 해낼 수 있을 거라고 믿어.

I bet you can make it.

16

May all your dreams come true!

May all your dreams come true! 너의 모든 꿈이 이루어지기를!

May all your dreams come true!

위로/격려의 편지

17

Stay strong and get well soon.

Stay strong and get well soon. 용기 잃지 마시고 빨리 회복하세요.

Stay strong and get well soon.

18

I am so sorry to hear about your loss.

I am so sorry to hear about your loss. 삼가 조의를 표합니다.

I am so sorry to hear about your loss.

19

I wish you success.

I wish you success. 좋은 성과가 있으시길 빌어요.

I wish you success.

20

I hope you are feeling better soon.

I hope you are feeling better soon. 건강이 좋아지시기를 바랍니다.

I hope you are feeling better soon.

영어 필기체 쉽게 쓰기 100문장
자유롭게 적어보기

영어 일기 필수 문장 20

하루의 시작 표현

1

It's time to wake up.

It's time to wake up. 일어날 시간이다.

It's time to wake up.

2

I need a cup of coffee every morning.

I need a cup of coffee every morning. 매일 아침 커피를 마셔야 한다.

I need a cup of coffee every morning.

3

I really like jogging in the morning.

I really like jogging in the morning. 아침에 조깅하는 것은 정말 좋다.

I really like jogging in the morning.

4

I want to rest.

I want to rest. 쉬고 싶다.

I want to rest.

기분/상태 표현

5

I think it's insomnia.

I think it's insomnia. 불면증인 것 같다.

I think it's insomnia.

6

I usually go to bed early.

I usually go to bed early. 나는 보통 일찍 자는 편이다.

I usually go to bed early.

7

I feel I'm getting better.

I feel I'm getting better. 몸이 나아지는 것 같다.

I feel I'm getting better.

8

It was a wonderful day today.

It was a wonderful day today. 오늘은 정말 즐거운 하루였다.

It was a wonderful day today.

일상 활동에 대한 표현

9

It's raining today.

It's raining today. 오늘은 비가 온다.

It's raining today.

10

I had a hamburger for lunch.

I had a hamburger for lunch. 나는 점심으로 햄버거를 먹었다.

I had a hamburger for lunch.

11

I went on a picnic.

I went on a picnic. 나는 소풍을 갔다.

I went on a picnic.

12

I've got a haircut.

I've got a haircut. 미용실에서 머리를 잘랐다.

I've got a haircut.

친구에 대한 표현

13 *We haven't met each other for a long time.*
We haven't met each other for a long time. 우리는 오랫동안 만나지 못했다.

We haven't met each other for a long time.

14 *I was so glad to meet him.*
I was so glad to meet him. 그를 만나서 정말 기뻤다.

I was so glad to meet him.

15 *I had some drinks with my friend.*
I had some drinks with my friend. 친구와 술을 한잔 했다.

I had some drinks with my friend.

16 *I think he's a real friend to me.*
I think he's a real friend to me. 난 그가 내 진정한 친구라고 생각한다.

I think he's a real friend to me.

사랑에 대한 표현

17

I'm dying to see her.

I'm dying to see her. 그녀가 보고 싶어 죽겠다.

I'm dying to see her.

18

I'm gonna ask her out tomorrow.

I'm gonna ask her out tomorrow. 내일 그녀에게 데이트 신청을 할 것이다.

I'm gonna ask her out tomorrow.

19

We went to the movies.

We went to the movies. 우리는 영화를 보러 갔다.

We went to the movies.

20

I was so happy to be with her today.

I was so happy to be with her today. 오늘 그녀와 함께할 수 있어서 정말 행복했다.

I was so happy to be with her today.

영어 필기체 쉽게 쓰기 100문장
자유롭게 적어보기

속담 및 격언 명문장 20

우정/사랑에 대하여

1
A friend in need is a friend indeed.
A friend in need is a friend indeed. 필요할 때 친구가 진짜 친구다.

A friend in need is a friend indeed.

2
A friend to all is a friend to none.
A friend to all is a friend to none. 모든 이의 친구는 누구의 친구도 아니다.

A friend to all is a friend to none.

3
We can only learn to love by loving.
We can only learn to love by loving. 오로지 사랑함으로써 사랑을 배울 수 있다.

We can only learn to love by loving.

4
Love is, above all else, the gift of oneself.
Love is, above all else, the gift of oneself. 사랑은 무엇보다도 자신을 위한 선물이다.

Love is, above all else, the gift of oneself.

지식에 대하여

5

Knowledge is power.

Knowledge is power. 아는 것이 힘이다.

Knowledge is power.

6

It's never too late to learn.

It's never too late to learn. 배움에 나이는 없다.

It's never too late to learn.

7

A rolling stone gathers no moss.

A rolling stone gathers no moss. 구르는 돌에는 이끼가 끼지 않는다.

A rolling stone gathers no moss.

8

Reading makes a full man.

Reading makes a full man. 독서가 사람을 완성한다.

Reading makes a full man.

삶의 지혜 1

9

All that glitters is not gold.

All that glitters is not gold. 반짝이는 모든 것이 다 금은 아니다.

All that glitters is not gold.

10

Art is long, life is short.

Art is long, life is short. 예술은 길고 인생은 짧다.

Art is long, life is short.

11

To see is to believe.

To see is to believe. 보는 것이 믿는 것이다.

To see is to believe.

12

Love truth, and pardon error.

Love truth, and pardon error. 진실을 사랑하고 실수를 용서하라.

Love truth, and pardon error.

삶의 지혜 2

13

Easy come, easy go.

Easy come, easy go. 쉽게 얻는 것은 쉽게 잃는다.

Easy come, easy go.

14

Better late than never.

Better late than never. 늦는 것이 안 하는 것보다 낫다.

Better late than never.

15

Well begun is half done.

Well begun is half done. 시작이 좋으면 반은 된 셈이다.

Well begun is half done.

16

Actions speak louder than words.

Actions speak louder than words. 말보다는 행동이 중요하다.

Actions speak louder than words.

희망에 대하여

17

Time heals all wounds.

Time heals all wounds. 시간이 약이다.

Time heals all wounds.

18

Hope is a waking dream.

Hope is a waking dream. 희망은 백일몽이다.

Hope is a waking dream.

19

Great hopes make great men.

Great hopes make great men. 큰 희망이 큰 사람을 만든다.

Great hopes make great men.

20

Hope is only the love of life.

Hope is only the love of life. 희망만이 인생을 사랑하는 유일한 것이다.

Hope is only the love of life.

영어 필기체 쉽게 쓰기 100문장
자유롭게 적어보기

명사들의 명언 쓰기 20

방송인/예술가

1 *Laughter is the tonic, the relief, the surcease for pain.*

Laughter is the tonic, the relief, the surcease for pain. 웃음은 강장제이고, 안정제이며, 진통제이다.
-Charlie Chaplin(찰리 채플린)

Laughter is the tonic, the relief, the surcease for pain.

2 *What we dwell on is who we become.*

What we dwell on is who we become. 우리가 무슨 생각을 하느냐가 어떤 사람이 되는지를 결정합니다.
-Oprah Winfrey(오프라 윈프리)

What we dwell on is who we become.

3 *Though the sun is gone, I have a light.*

Though the sun is gone, I have a light. 비록 태양이 사라져도 나는 한 줄기 빛을 얻으리라. -Kurt Cobain(커트 코베인)

Though the sun is gone, I have a light.

4 *Miracles happen to those who believe in them.*

Miracles happen to those who believe in them. 기적은 기적을 믿는 자에게 일어난다.
-Bernard Berenson(버나드 베렌슨)

Miracles happen to those who believe in them.

사업가/과학자

5

The journey is the reward.

The journey is the reward. 여정은 (목적지로 향하는 과정이지만, 그 자체로) 보상이다. -Steve Jobs(스티브 잡스)

The journey is the reward.

6

I'm as proud of what we don't do as I am of what we do.

I'm as proud of what we don't do as I am of what we do. 우리가 이룬 것만큼 이루지 못한 것도 자랑스럽습니다.
-Steve Jobs(스티브 잡스)

I'm as proud of what we don't do as I am of what we do.

7

Knowledge is love and light and vision.

Knowledge is love and light and vision. 지식은 사랑이요, 빛이며 통찰력이다. -Helen Keller(헬렌 켈러)

Knowledge is love and light and vision.

8

Only a life lived of others is a life worth while.

Only a life lived of others is a life worth while. 오직 남을 위해 산 인생만이 가치 있다.
-Albert Einstein(알버트 아인슈타인)

Only a life lived of others is a life worth while.

성인

9

Intense love does not measure, it just gives.

Intense love does not measure, it just gives. 사랑은 판단하지 않는다, 주기만 할 뿐. -Mother Teresa(마더 테레사)

Intense love does not measure, it just gives.

10

Hate the sin, love the sinner.

Hate the sin, love the sinner. 죄는 미워하되, 죄인은 사랑하라. -Mahatma Gandhi(마하트마 간디)

Hate the sin, love the sinner.

11

Live simply that others may simply live.

Live simply that others may simply live. 남들이 단순하게 살 수 있도록 단순하게 살라. -Mahatma Gandhi(마하트마 간디)

Live simply that others may simply live.

12

The hardest work is to go die.

The hardest work is to go die. 가장 하기 힘든 일은 아무 일도 안 하는 것이다. -유대인 격언

The hardest work is to go die.

작가

13

A friend in power is a friend lost.

A friend in power is a friend lost. 힘 있을 때 친구는 친구가 아니다. -Henry Adams(헨리 애덤스)

A friend in power is a friend lost.

14

He who has never hoped can never despair.

He who has never hoped can never despair. 희망을 품지 않은 자는 절망도 할 수 없다.
-George Bernard Shaw(조지 버나드 쇼)

He who has never hoped can never despair.

15

Where there is great love there are always miracles.

Where there is great love there are always miracles. 커다란 사랑이 있는 곳에는 언제나 기적이 존재한다.
-Willa Cather(윌라 캐더)

Where there is great love there are always miracles.

16

Every cubic inch of space is a miracle.

Every cubic inch of space is a miracle. 우주에 기적이 아닌 것은 없다. -Walt Whitman(월트 휘트먼)

Every cubic inch of space is a miracle.

정치인/교육자

17

He that lives upon hope will die fasting.

He that lives upon hope will die fasting. 희망만을 먹고 사는 자는 굶어 죽을 것이다.
-Benjamin Franklin(벤자민 프랭클린)

He that lives upon hope will die fasting.

18

Early morning hath gold in its mouth.

Early morning hath gold in its mouth. 이른 아침은 입에 황금을 물고 있다. -Benjamin Franklin(벤자민 프랭클린)

Early morning hath gold in its mouth.

19

The empires of the future are the empires of the mind.

The empires of the future are the empires of the mind. 미래의 제국은 마음의 제국이다.
-Sir Winston Churchill(윈스턴 처칠)

The empires of the future are the empires of the mind.

20

The first duty of love is to listen.

The first duty of love is to listen. 사랑의 첫 번째 의무는 상대방에 귀 기울이는 것이다. -Paul Tillich(폴 틸리히)

The first duty of love is to listen.

영어 필기체 쉽게 쓰기 100문장
자유롭게 적어보기

영어필기체쉽게쓰기100문장

문학작품 써보기

William Shakespeare
셰익스피어 작품 명문장 1

- Love looks not with the eyes, but with the mind.
- Our bodies are our gardens to which our wills are gardeners.
- O, how this spring of love resembleth
  The uncertain glory of an April day!
- To be or not to be, that is a problem.
- Frailty, thy name is woman!
- There's no art to find the mind's construction in the face.
- Things without all remedy should be without regard;
  what's done is done.

- Love looks not with the eyes, but with the mind.
- Our bodies are our gardens to which our wills are gardeners.
- O, how this spring of love resembleth
  The uncertain glory of an April day!
- To be or not to be, that is a problem.
- Frailty, thy name is woman!
- There's no art to find the mind's construction in the face.
- Things without all remedy should be without regard;
  what's done is done.

- 사랑은 눈으로 보지 않고 마음으로 보는 거지.
- 우리의 몸은 정원이요, 우리의 의지는 정원사다.
- 아, 이 사랑의 봄은 사월 어느 날의 변덕스런 영광을 닮았구나!
- 죽느냐 사느냐, 그것이 문제로다.
- 약한 자여 그대 이름은 여자로다!
- 얼굴만 보고는 마음의 본성을 알 수 없다.
- 어찌할 수 없는 일은 잊을 수밖에 없다. 지나간 일은 지나간 일이다.

한 번 쓰기

두 번 쓰기

William Shakespeare
셰익스피어 작품 명문장 2

- Silence is the perfectest herald of joy:
  I were but little happy, if I could say how much.

- Glory is like a circle in the water, which never ceaseth to enlarge itself,
  till by broad spreading it disperses to naught.

- Be not afraid of greatness: some men are born great,
  some achieve greatness and some have greatness thrust upon them.

- When griping grief the heart doth wound,
  and doleful dumps the mind opresses,
  then music, with her silver sound,
  with speedy help doth lend redress.

- Silence is the perfectest herald of joy:
  I were but little happy, if I could say how much.
- Glory is like a circle in the water, which never ceaseth to enlarge itself,
  till by broad spreading it disperses to naught.
- Be not afraid of greatness: some men are born great,
  some achieve greatness and some have greatness thrust upon them.
- When griping grief the heart doth wound,
  and doleful dumps the mind opresses,
  then music, with her silver sound,
  with speedy help doth lend redress.

- 침묵이야말로 기쁨을 전하는 최고의 전령이지요. 말로 할 수 있는 정도의 기쁨이라면 대수롭지 않은 것이지요.
- 영광이란 수면에 퍼지는 파문과 같은 것, 점점 넓게 퍼져 사라질 때까지 계속 커지지.
- 위대함을 두려워 말라. 어떤 사람은 위대하게 태어나고, 어떤 사람은 위대함을 성취하며,
  그리고 어떤 사람들은 그들에게 위대함을 떠맡긴다.
- 고통스러운 슬픔으로 가슴에 상처를 입고 슬픔에 마음이 혼란스러울 때, 음악은 은빛 화음으로 빠르게 치유의
  손길을 내민다.

한 번 쓰기

두 번 쓰기

William Shakespeare
셰익스피어 작품 명문장 3

- Men must endure
  Their going hence, even as their coming hither:
  Ripeness is all.

- Poor and content is rich, and rich enough,
  But riches, fineless, is as poor as winter
  To him that ever fears he shall be poor.

- Love is a smoke made with the fume of sighs,
  being purged, a fire sparkling in lovers eyes,
  Being vexed, a sea nourished with lovers tears.
  What is it else? A madness most discreet,
  A choking gall and a preserving sweet.

- Men must endure
  Their going hence, even as their coming hither:
  Ripeness is all.
- Poor and content is rich, and rich enough,
  But riches, fineless, is as poor as winter
  To him that ever fears he shall be poor.
- Love is a smoke made with the fume of sighs,
  being purged, a fire sparkling in lovers eyes,
  Being vexed, a sea nourished with lovers tears.
  What is it else? A madness most discreet,
  A choking gall and a preserving sweet.

- 사람은 참아야 한다. 이 세상을 떠날 때나, 이 세상에 태어날 때나. 때가 무르익는 것이 중요하다.
- 가난해도 족함을 알면 백만장자가 부럽지 않지만,
  아무리 부자라 한들 가난뱅이가 되면 어떡하나 하고 걱정만 한다면, 엄동설한 같이 쓸쓸하기 그지없다.
- 사랑이란 한숨으로 일으켜지는 연기, 개면 애인 눈 속에서 번쩍이는 불꽃이요,
  흐리면 애인 눈물로 바다가 되네. 그게 사랑 아닌가?
  가장 분별 있는 미치광이요, 또한 목을 졸라매는 쓰디쓴 약인가 하면, 생명에 활력을 주는 감로이기도 하네.

한 번 쓰기

두 번 쓰기

The Little Prince
어린왕자 1

"If someone loves a flower, of which just one single blossom grows in all the millions and millions of stars, it is enough to make him happy just to look at the stars. He can say to himself, 'Somewhere, my flower is there...' But if the sheep eats the flower, in one moment all his stars will be darkened... And you think that is not important!"

"If someone loves a flower, of which just one single blossom
grows in all the millions and millions of stars,
it is enough to make him happy just to look at the stars.
He can say to himself, 'Somewhere, my flower is there…'
But if the sheep eats the flower,
in one moment all his stars will be darkened…
And you think that is not important!"

"수백 만 개의 별들 중에 단 하나밖에 존재하지 않는 꽃을 사랑하고 있는 사람은 그 별들을 바라보고 있는 것만으로 행복할 수 있어. 그는 속으로 '내 꽃이 저기 어딘가에 있겠지…' 하고 생각할 수 있거든.
하지만 양이 그 꽃을 먹는다면 그에게는 갑자기 모든 별들이 사라져 버리게 되는 거나 마찬가지야…
그런데도 그게 중요하지 않다는 거지?"
그는 더 말을 잇지 못했다. 그는 별안간 흐느껴 울기 시작했다.

한 번 쓰기

두 번 쓰기

The Little Prince
어린왕자 2

"And what do you do with them?"
"I administer them," replied the businessman.
"I count them and recount them. It is difficult.
But I am a man who is naturally interested in matters of consequence."
The little prince was still not satisfied.
"If I owned a silk scarf," he said,
"I could put it around my neck and take it away with me.
If I owned a flower, I could pluck that flower and take it away with me. But you cannot pluck the stars from heaven…"

"And what do you do with them?"
"I administer them," replied the businessman.
"I count them and recount them. It is difficult.
But I am a man who is naturally interested in matters of consequence."
The little prince was still not satisfied.
"If I owned a silk scarf," he said,
"I could put it around my neck and take it away with me.
If I owned a flower, I could pluck that flower and take it away with me. But you cannot pluck the stars from heaven…"

"아저씨는 별들을 가지고 뭘 해?"
"그것들을 관리하지. 세어 보고 또 세어 보고 하지. 그건 힘든 일이야. 하지만 나는 진지한 사람이거든!"
어린 왕자는 그래도 흡족해 하지 않았다.
"나는 말이야, 머플러를 소유하고 있을 때는 그것을 목에 두르고 다닐 수가 있어.
또 꽃을 소유하고 있을 때는 그 꽃을 꺾어 가지고 다닐 수가 있고. 하지만 아저씨는 별들을 꺾을 수가 없잖아…"

한 번 쓰기

두 번 쓰기

The Little Prince
어린왕자 3

"She would be very much annoyed,"
he said to himself,
"if she should see that... she would cough most dreadfully,
and she would pretend that she was dying,
to avoid being laughed at.
And I should be obliged to pretend that
I was nursing her back to life—
for if I did not do that, to humble myself also,
she would really allow herself to die..."

"She would be very much annoyed,"
he said to himself,
"if she should see that… she would cough most dreadfully,
and she would pretend that she was dying,
to avoid being laughed at.
And I should be obliged to pretend that I was nursing her back to life–
for if I did not do that, to humble myself also, she would really allow herself to die…"

"내 꽃이 이걸 보면 몹시 상심할 거야" 하고 어린 왕자는 스스로에게 말했다.
"기침을 지독히 해대면서 창피한 모습을 보이지 않으려고 죽는 시늉을 할 거야.
그럼 난 간호해 주는 척하지 않을 수 없겠지.
그러지 않으면 내게 죄책감을 주려고 정말로 죽어 버릴지도 몰라…"

한 번 쓰기

두 번 쓰기

The Little Prince
어린왕자 4

"To me, you are still nothing more than a little boy who is just like a hundred thousand other little boys.
And I have no need of you.
And you, on your part, have no need of me.
To you, I am nothing more than a fox like a hundred thousand other foxes.
But if you tame me, then we shall need each other.
To me, you will be unique in all the world.
To you, I shall be unique in all the world..."

"To me, you are still nothing more than a little boy who is
just like a hundred thousand other little boys.
And I have no need of you. And you, on your part, have no need of me.
To you, I am nothing more than a fox like a hundred
thousand other foxes.
But if you tame me, then we shall need each other.
To me, you will be unique in all the world.
To you, I shall be unique in all the world…"

"넌 아직 나에겐 다른 수많은 소년들과 다를 바 없는 소년이야. 그래서 난 너를 필요로 하지 않지.
네 입장에서는 나를 필요로 하지 않겠지. 난 너에겐 수많은 다른 여우와 다를 게 없으니까.
하지만 네가 나를 길들인다면 우린 서로를 필요로 하게 될 거야.
나에게 너는 세상 단 하나밖에 없는 존재가 될 거야. 너에게 나도 이 세상에 오직 하나뿐인 존재가 되겠지…"

한 번 쓰기

두 번 쓰기

The Little Prince
어린왕자 5

"If, for example, you come at four o'clock in the afternoon, then at three o'clock I shall begin to be happy. I shall feel happier and happier as the hour advances. At four o'clock, I shall already be worrying and jumping about. I shall show you how happy I am! But if you come at just any time, I shall never know at what hour my heart is to be ready to greet you… One must observe the proper rites…"

"If, for example, you come at four o'clock in the afternoon, then at three o'clock I shall begin to be happy. I shall feel happier and happier as the hour advances. At four o'clock, I shall already be worrying and jumping about. I shall show you how happy I am! But if you come at just any time, I shall never know at what hour my heart is to be ready to greet you… One must observe the proper rites…"

"이를테면, 네가 오후 네 시에 온다면 난 세 시부터 행복해지기 시작할 거야.
시간이 갈수록 난 점점 더 행복해지겠지. 네 시에는 흥분해서 안절부절 못 할 거야.
그러면 행복이 얼마나 값진 것인가 알게 되겠지!
아무 때나 오면 몇 시에 마음을 곱게 단장을 해야 하는지 모르잖아. 의식이 필요하거든."

한 번 쓰기

두 번 쓰기

예쁜 필기체 써보기

Thank you always being my friend!
Thank you always being my friend! 항상 나의 친구로 있어 줘서 고마워!

Merry Christmas and Happy New Year!
Merry Christmas and Happy New Year! 즐거운 성탄과 행복한 새해되세요!

Happy holidays.
Happy holidays. 행복한 연휴되세요.

I can't stop thinking about you.
I can't stop thinking about you. 나는 당신 생각을 멈출 수가 없어요.

I love you more than anything.
I love you more than anything. 난 너를 세상 무엇보다 사랑해.

I love you with all my heart.
I love you with all my heart. 나는 당신을 진심으로 사랑해요.

Best wishes for your 20th birthday.
Best wishes for your 20th Birthday. 20번째 생일을 축하해.

I wish you a happy Teachers' Day.
I wish you a happy Teachers' Day. 행복한 스승의 날 되시기 바랍니다.

You are the best teacher in this world.
You are the best teacher in this world. 선생님은 세상 최고의 선생님이십니다.